Small Stories

Janice Starck

A selection of modern poetry

Abundance Communications | Kuranda

Copyright © 2025 by Janice Starck

All rights reserved. No part of this publication may be reproduced, distributed or transmitted in any form or by any means, without prior written permission.

Janice Starck/Abundance Communications
PO BOX 444
Kuranda, Queensland 4881

Publisher's Note: This is a work of fiction. Names, characters, places, and incidents are a product of the author's imagination. Locales and public names are sometimes used for atmospheric purposes. Any resemblance to actual people, living or dead, or to businesses, companies, events, institutions, or locales is completely coincidental.

Book Layout © 2017 BookDesignTemplates.com

Small Stories/ Janice Starck. -- 1st ed.
ISBN 978-0-6487361-2-7

Dedicated to my children Bun, Fred and Bucky.

Contents

SYDNEY	7
DANGER	8
SYDNEY RUSH HOUR AND A RUN IN WITH POLICE	9
THE JOB	11
WAVES	13
SHINING THROUGH THE SMOKESCREEN	14
PADDY'S PIAZZA	15
THE BEACH BAR	17
SEA WIFE	18
LOCAL LABOUR	19
PAINTING THE IDEAL MAN	21
CITIZENSHIP	22
FAREWELL	23
ONE LAST DRINK	24
RECYCLED WOOD	25
OLD DOG	26
JUST US	28
NARCOSIS OF THE DEEP	30
THE WINDOW	31
MARKET STALLS FOR RENT	32
TO VELCRO	34
OUTRIGGER	35

HABITUATION	36
I AM MUM! (A slam poem)	37
HAIKUS FOR AUNTY	39
MY ANCHOR	41
AUNTY'S DOG	43
SUN BIRDS	45
MISSING YOU	46
INFINITESIMAL	47
MYSTIC MEETING	48
THE SUN	49
TURMERIC IN OIL	50
WISH BONE IN WAITING	51
SLEEP	53
MY BOTANY PROFESSOR	54
MY UNCLE IN SPRING	55
AFTER GLOW	56
THE USUAL SUSPECTS	57
SUNDAY WALKING	58
LEARNING TO DANCE AGAIN	59
COMMUNION	61
LONE GRAVE	62
LIKE CHOCOLATE FOR LOVE	63
TOURISM	64
MEETING MY MOTHER	67
NIGHT DIVE ON THE REEF	68
THE DRESSMAKER	69
THE NIGHT IS OVER	71

CANCER CURE	75
HALLOWEEN	77
GOODNIGHT	78

SYDNEY

Suddenly I'm here. 1976
the gleaming expanse ahead.
Sydney from a beat-up ute
Growling into the maze
of architecture from another time
Another mindset and another people.
Sorry about the rattle of nuts and bolts
Hang on tight, my driver roared.
We laughed, fuelling the old wreck home.
Auckland to Sydney. It felt exotic.
With a surge of delight and newness
We clattered to the North Shore.
Sun warmer and sea brighter.
Was it just the change or reality?
That Sydney outshone Auckland.
Life was suddenly expanding.
Bigger, brighter and beefier.
The harbour, like a Thomas Wattling
painting on steroids. I'm here.
My mates all preceded me!
They said there were jobs galore.
Hopes gluttonous beyond belief.
Sydney, a name, a story, a vacuum.

DANGER

It was summer and a new latitude of warmth.
No one mentioned the hidden dangers.
The natural history and the evolution of toxins,
tactics and terror. I was a Kiwi wearing a cloak
of ignorance for protection. We were such fun.

How they teased and how we squealed.
Fun did rear its constant head and the heart
of the city felt kind and my friends protective.
All this stripped bare and cruelly raped
when I met the funnel web on the floor.

It's just a spider! OK New Zealand has spiders.
With no more history than last night's dinner.
This is insane. Funnel webs are so very toxic!
They shrugged. Yes, death is a notable side effect.
How proud they are. It leads the world in toxicity.

My anxiety meter has jammed and my bladder
threatens a deluge of biblical proportions.
A human male of muscles, stealth and swagger
oozes confidence with cologne and white teeth,
A glint of a smile and a charm to cool the creeps.

I see a broom and a flick and hear a drum roll.
The Arachnid hurtles out the door, the kids jump.
They laugh like seasoned saviours which they were.
What happened to that hovering handsome man?
Did I see the Marlborough man or an eye-brain scam?

SYDNEY RUSH HOUR AND A RUN IN WITH POLICE

Fresh from New Zealand
Weird smells ooze with
oil, petrol and people.

Sydney Town's insane
Rush that was exciting
Blasphemous and free.

I was insecure, slightly
Shadow scared and my
upbringing gave no help.

Lost? Go ask a policeman.
Always stolid wearing a
helmet and truncheon.

Servants of the people.
But Constable Plod it seems,
stays firmly in New Zealand.

I found a policeman. Sunnies
tight clothes, packing a gun.
Hat, no helmet or a smile.

Where is Queen Street Sir?
Manner's matter. He glared.

'Do you think I'm a tour guide?'

He glanced annoyed for a sign.
To my absolute Kiwi delight
we were standing in it.

THE JOB

A new dream job. Sydney harbour.
Unexpected and more than I hoped.
I left a country where jobs were
crudely stamped and illogically male.
I thought, why would they hire me?
So, I applied anyway. Diving yes,
research yes. Marine biology
assuredly yes and medically fit.

I met the team all girls and no man.
Is something up? My thoughts alert
Our boss, definitely male, off we go.
The outboards snorting their tails.
Dinghies loaded to the gunnels as we
 ran beyond the harbour and the heads
To open ocean and brave specks of
fishermen on the wave crashing rocks.

I breathed the adventure of the ocean.
Girls together and a quiet trusty boss.
We dived, we ramset, we counted
Measured, collected, filmed, wrote on
white plastic and with numbing fingers
collected our gear and home to the lab.
Identify, weigh, and write each story.
A precision day and a Boss to die for.
Was our femininity a choice?
Were we first cabs off the ranks?
Was it someone else's doing?
Big breath. Why Girls? I ventured.

His answer, novel, unexpected.
'I'm sick of men,' he shrugged
'Telling me how to do my job'
Ah Sydney! An unexpected love.

WAVES

Across the bay they dribble
In meek orderly rows
With sharp little tips
Waiting for a gust of wind
To curl their edges in a smile.

At the heads the open ocean
Lends power to the young
Waves with fingers curling
Whites showing and hoping
To cause fear in our eyes.

The barometer is powerless
Today. The slap and thump
Are nothing more than music.
The wind, a mere edgy chorus
The sun gently warms our sighs.

Tanks and weight belts clang
A clumsy entry into the cold rush
Of water oozing in our suits
Remind us of the job to do.
Ready and willing, down we go.

Our plates packed with crusty life
Enjoy the current that feeds them.
The deep swells growing beneath
Promise a rough happy trip home,
As the data builds like the waves.

SHINING THROUGH THE SMOKESCREEN

The Kiwi accent.

I blame the Scots! 'A wee but.'
This didn't describe my bottom
Or my urinal incontinence.
It does lay blame in one direction
We can always blame the Poms
Because they have a scapegoat
And try to blame the Cockneys.
Then the South Easterners cop
Some flak for being closer to us.

I thought being from Christchurch
Would lend a small hope of posh
To my disease-ridden vowels and
If I half shut my mouth in a mumble
And merge consonants and verbs
As rapidly as troops with no leader,
Would I still 'putch my tint in a dup?
With a dick chair beside my jandles,
If I promise to order fush and chups.'

I thought Yes! So, I fancy up my vowels,
Have a scintillating exchange plus smiles,
While I drop a few endings with hob knob
Inflection, some rounded O's, a bit of Irish
It's always demoralising after an effusive chat
 when they assuredly say, 'so you're a Kiwi!'
The hysteria continues when I look aghast,
And say with naïve shock. 'How can you tell?'

PADDY'S PIAZZA

Behind the dead train tracks on a broken brick laneway
somewhere in Glebe, it could be the moon, no one cares.
Are six worker's cottages someone must collect rent for.
Sagging a dozen steps from the road where no cars drive.
Named because an old man had deep memories of Italy.

A friendly oddball ghetto with nothing to hear but gossip
and sometimes a lecture from a long-retired tradesman.
The rough of crumbling veranda, chair legs stuck in cracks,
an old carpenter who settles for physics and not design
eyes the rift and sag of floor and chuckles at its strength.

A student, long hair, duffel coat and a head of dreams
the old boys mess with but respect his brains and vision.
He talks mechanics, heads nod a memory from the clouds.
They feel in good hands with this oddity from another place.
Paying with beers, cheap wine and promises of dirty jokes.

Few pass by the Piazza as it only leads to cheap dreams
in the decaying cottages and gardens not yet condemned.
The meagre gardens still spawn bullet proof garden herbs.
Life has its golden moments when a beauty with laundry
and food from Mum visits Mr. Hirsute who shares his
largesse.

The Piazza becomes festive when stew, mashed spud and
peas
garnish the angular table where the old boys ooze polite talk
from a time before. She thinks they are sweet and
gentlemanly

and wishes her generation were the same. On these occasions
wars, atrocities, deprivation and current news sink behind joy.

THE BEACH BAR

A beach bar so low key and romantic
Best visited at dusk while the sun burns low
Cooling the bay as it darkens to teasing golden hues.
Across drunken tables, wet, uneven, covered in windblown sand
The staff gather and pamper them for happy hour to reset nearer the bar.
We arrive, damp in bikinis, wet T-shirts and nipples hijacking decency with salt water.

We slouch, smelling of frangipanni in oil.
Island sarongs with hibiscus and teasing tassels.
Glints of blonde hair damaged beyond repair and brown skin
Adding to wrinkles promise as we languish and order beers and dreams.
The old locals look on, we are polite and smile and nod a greeting in their territory.
Do they see exquisite tans bleached hair of every shade, pretty faces with gleaming teeth?

Do they see beauty that has a lot to learn, or ignorant youth where age is a looming reality.
The sun sets on all of us, our laughs tinkle and the patrons fade into the dusk after skinfuls
of happy juice, mixed memories, raucous laughs, lustful gazes and hopefully, no regrets.

SEA WIFE

She offers her land bound heart
To the man whose love only knows
The curl of the ocean's shapes
And the shadows of night teasing
Gestures and images like her.

He returns some Nereus she imagines
But gaunt as the trawler takings.
A season of angry spume and spent muscle.
While gifts he showers upon her
Like memories in spring.

The dance of vagrant ripples
Bursting like fledgling waves
Mothered by dolphins
And tempered by the wind.
His love is always there.

She is always there waiting like the
Brown path through the green field
To the gate with its rash red on blue
Where the sun curls its lonely fingers
Around her heart until he returns.

LOCAL LABOUR

The grass they say is never greener
 in the next town
Nor as coloured as my senses
As green as new growth.
Michelangelo, they add, was a mere
 apprentice in all manner of design
And their keen perception
And well-honed sense of real matters
Lay concerns and overtime to rest.
They arrive at the job, eagerly
Armed with weapons of their trade.
With hammer near enough in hand
Carthage falls by lunchtime.
The smack of abandoned tools
Echo the whips that bend
The miserable hoards
To construct another pyramid
Grander than Cheops
Come smoko an Obelisk
 to dwarf the best in Egypt.
Plaster glints with precious stones
While the eye checks for parallax
In the Taj Mahal, as Babylon
Is landscaped in a flash.
By five o'clock Cain is razed
And London bridge stands glorious.
Genghis Khan receives directives
Punctuated by the sweep of another joint
Subtending a squinting countenance
Behind some Smokey camouflage.

With the adulation of kings and queens
The pub doors crash open to a rousing cheer
Visigoths line the bar the vandals wait outside.
Nectar! The gods yell and liquor flows.
Sword arms hang unencumbered
At the ready to pat the barmaid's arse.
While out in the street's arena
Chariots charge, lights flashing
Ben Hur yells, abandon all vehicles
Abandon all hope and don't blow.
Crashes and the arena doors clang shut.
The locks? Mere chastity belts
But the damsel looks uninviting
With a gun and dressed in blue.

PAINTING THE IDEAL MAN

I can't see you on any canvas
Because I haven't met you yet.
At times you are bright blobs of reason
Merging into infrequent runs of colour
When they are being kind and helpful.
But I do like spots of winking metallics
Speckling nonchalantly down the frame.
To embody you in colour and feelings
Leaping like a rainbow's curved shape.
I need to speak to you in gentle gibberish
And see the perfect resume with face
Perhaps a form might help fill the void.
But unconquerable rears its ugly head
Along with a difficult, dangerous, dewy,
 sleepy eyed brain losing consciousness.
The night intercedes and takes my mind
On a fantasy journey. 'Goodnight, World.'

CITIZENSHIP

Queensland forty years ago
I became a fair dinkum Aussie.
Australia Day, bustling crowds
The park decked out in garlands
And the band was a ripsnorter.
Dresses fit for Country Vogue
And a happy bunch of newbies
Packed the solid pop-up stage
As we waited for the mayor.
G'Day he said. Ready to go!
In tobacco and cattle country
With farms of flowers and fruit
Veggies to die for, sugar cane
Grains and home cooking.
Smiles expansive and everywhere.
All this accompanied our declaration
Boldly read, giving our loyalty to
Her Majesty Queen Elizabeth II.
We gave it our best volume and
Best English which differed somewhat.
It was a bit of a dog's breakfast
But the end result in a town whose
Signage made the heart laugh.
Thank you for smoking
And as a reminder to us all,
Give the man meat.
There was no pulling the wool
Over our eyes as we became one
With a town that made us Australian Citizens

FAREWELL

The final plunge Tu Meke
Into the river's swift playful grab.
You join the many spent
Peals of laughter and ribald insults
For your catch of sooty grunters
Smaller than half a hand.

We pour you, silvered specks of ash
Curling and folding in the afternoon breeze
As the sun in the river rightly dims
You roil and boil like a shark
Then merge into the river's liquid arms.

You never came to conquer the river
Nor fish the biggest scaled beast
Because you never came alone
You came with me.
Did the river absorb our laughter?
Did it remember your foolish catches
and laugh with us, or was it the beer
and tea and an old camp chair
you always carried for me?
Farewell my love, your liquid Haka
Will dance you out to sea.

ONE LAST DRINK

When intoxicated - mostly in another's eyes!
  Staggering lame and arrogant
To an inevitable fate of waning liquor
You look desperately for a small tipple.
Smoke and food are not a substitute.
  You flail and demand another drink
Ignore the heartless care on other faces
They are fools in the scheme of things.
Food! Such an anathema to a full stomach
  Already burdened with the juice of greed.
Another drink won't impede your fate
Which could be bed companions of bushes
Or the street on a cold winter's night
  Let's hope a friendship might be ignited
In a half blind damsel coercing you
Into a bed three sheets to the wind, where your
Legless entry might end in mutual impairment.

RECYCLED WOOD

There's a warmth in recycled wood
Weathered and dry from years
In the sun and fun in the shade
To render it passive and easy.
The wood lives another day
As it staves off rot and lichen frills
Uninvited cancers of fungi
Saprophytic bullies recycle
The wood into its own being.
It thumbs at white ants when
Saved by the carpenter God.
With paint, shelter and care
Nailed fast, a demi-god itself
In the war against waste.

OLD DOG

Slow and calm as the summer hollows
Ben shambles serenely
Offering the brittle snaps of his life
To the leguminous pods, and the
Foes of many encounters to the
Beasts of his illusions.

His life is easy. It was earned.
Eyes, the only cataract in his being
Sense the harmonies of loves and strangers
The vibration from a scented bitch
Stir only his memory
And a few token thumps of a tired tail.

No cat seeks a short cut through his yard.
No dog an entrance
And no foul human sweat
Passes without a death snarl.
Yet, 'Menace' is his master's child.
As dangerous as a life of dog fights.

Eyes poked with little sticks
Nostrils reamed, ears crinkled
Like lolly papers, ribs rolled
And pummelled to blast
The last wheeze from his old chest.

Soulfully his mouth puckers
In a wet gummy grin
Quivering in time with tailbeat

Rhythms of his spirit
Reflecting the smile of ecstasy and peace.

JUST US

I'm child- sitting
a small girl, button
bright and eager.

Such a talker, words
beyond her years
and so assured.

She looked up. Let's
Sit. Just you and me
on those clouds.

They're like smoke
must be soft as feathers
She clutched herself.

Would there be fairies?
I whispered my attempt
to fit in.

That's ice cream
she pointed aloft.
Fairies love ice-cream.

I asked, is it cold?
She looked knowing.
We could think warm.

Let's sit on the clouds.
Her arms wave in a

merry greeting.

I ventured. Would
we fall through?
'Course not, she giggled.

We would float,
'cos it would be
just Us.

NARCOSIS OF THE DEEP

The now familiar tingling in the skin
is a meter to the brain of water depth
And a cloak of danger, wrapping comfort
from the blue cold and festive creatures.

Years back the deep cold kelp waters
from the south would boil and sting the skin
With feelings of false warmth and reverie
like dolphin calls in a ping of bubbles.

The lightness, free fall of the body
alien, alone, yet snuggly safe in a vault
Where jewels beckon in the shaft of light
sinking out of touch as your leaden senses.

Empathy. The heart of each breath shared
needlessly. The fluorescent creatures, wink
Their placards of salty warnings, tasting
of sugar, candy-coloured glints of scale.

Limbs flail rapturous with nitrogen
but respond at last to the warrior's heart
Another survival thrown away like used air
with the sobering breath of the land.

THE WINDOW

Glass flows.
I wish it could grab
quick passing images
in minute traces.
Could it capture
a flash of beauty?
Or hold the liquid sky
swimming in its tide
of precious images?
Sliding away unsolved
unable to grasp
the incompatible ooze.
Uncaptured visions
reflect like a slap.
They slide through
momentarily alive
then teleport away
like a brittle memory.

MARKET STALLS FOR RENT

Dear Sir/Madam,

It is with some trepidation
But much desire
I wish to hire a stall.

Their facades quaint and pleasing
To a person who knows well
The knocked-up humpy
And lean-to shed.

Also, a background nurturing
A quiet condition
Of natural solitude.

I shall weather the droughts
Of humans and floods
Of rain and occasional people.

I will not be disappointed.
I have an inner reserve born of
Squatting and starvation.

I also have some hidden energy
To deal with sometimes throngs
Like galahs in season
And lorikeets squabbling
Like mismatched siblings.

My psyche is fit for your

Glorious establishment
If in times of drought
We band together and laugh
And share our wealth of fun
With the ghosts whispering
A sense of impermanence
I will prevail.

Yours sincerely,

TO VELCRO

Today, odes to West Winds and
Grecian Urns seem pointless.
Perhaps an ode to lethargy might
Be apt or perhaps melancholy.
Technological marvels should
Be justly considered first.
Velcro. Claws and hooks forever
At the ready and opportunistically
Grabbing by evil default.
Pilling other delicate weaves
Stupid by its lack of recognition
Of its own mindless fuzzy half.
Aged, it loses grip to loosely hang
Like fairy floss holding on to an
Arthritic hook, medically impossible.
No substance or even function now.
Its once strong kiss weakens
Into a slack mouthed drool
That attempts to stick in patches
One last stand of defiance,
Until the islands of weakness
Crumble and succumb to death.
No longer glorified, once victorious
Now the victim of abuse and
Verbal rudeness as it is cast
Into the wheelie bin of despair.
You have ruined all hope of apparel.

OUTRIGGER

Our outrigger has its own heart
As it glides about the bay,
with its old sarong sail
Catching the breeze like us.
Creeping slowly to nowhere
Making shade in patches
As a whisp of wind moves the
Sun around our sail.
Our platform, of fronds
And towels, is cool and safe
Our chance direction is
Steady as our intent to be alone
You, the captain of our journey
To anywhere, while we sail
The two of us together.

HABITUATION

The sparrows know me.
I'm an oddity
Of shape and size
That they compute.
I'm under orders
To feed crumbs to
Fat frozen bellies.
Cold mornings they
Puff like meringues
At the doorstep.
Their memories huge,
Yesterday and the
Day before, become
Today and tomorrow.
Bread, I cast net-like
As old Aunty calls out,
Did you wet it first?
They just might choke.
Today is freezing
The birds, puffed and
Begging, get soggy
Bread as usual.
Soaking in Aunties love.

I AM MUM! (A slam poem)

I am Mum! This is true.
Ho Hum so are millions of others.
This is good. I have an army.
An army of every known rank to man.
I was a Field Marshal once. The fights
The tears, the near-death experiences,
The clutching at straws, quivering jaws
Until the oranges come out at half time.
As a General with a big mouth and
Fighting talk, I would wade into the fray
When Matilda gets her knuckles ripped
And Billy gets trodden into the mud
Along with his spectacles all in bits.
While the biggest bully, my son
Who can slay dragons, gets stiff armed
Back home to clean up his mess
And acknowledge civilisation for
A brief and foggy period of time.

I'm good cannon fodder, I have many skills.
I duck and weave, I lie low, I run for cover
Fire off a few shots and wait for sublime
Orders which never come.
When it's every man for himself
I summon my inner Sergeant Major,
I bellow orders left and right and
Insubordination is dealt with swiftly.

After the war when the smoke clears
And bellies are full and muscles dissolve

Into a higher consciousness,
Niceness and order might prevail.
There's satisfaction dangling on the end
Of a super strong thread and winning.
It looks frail and weak but it's an illusion.
It is stronger than life itself. Trust in your
Hard wiring and your military might.
Remember your exalted rank at the end
Of the day, at the end of another year,
At the end of another decade and beyond.
You are still a Mum.

HAIKUS FOR AUNTY

My very old aunt sleeps
Testing her dreams for treason.
Soul thieves in the night.

I saw my aunt's fear
Born of sickness and her loss
Youth, children and life.

She hoped her demons
Were just playthings in the mix
Just fun for a day.

She's old and cautious
But she knows when spring is here
New life and new love.

There's a smell of growth
It's a new way of living
When old senses die.

She lives with the spirit
Warm in the softest of seas
Salty in wisdom.

Its amniotic
And with her sharp pulsing mind
Life dances in step.
Wisdom drifts both ways
Faint breath, so soft on a whim
She sighs out a thought.

She has her own faith
It has always served her well
She knows God abides.

Soul thieves are glitches
She is safe with her prayers
And the whole Earth sings.

When her time is done
She knows there's only paradise
Because she has faith.

MY ANCHOR

I think I know the sea.
I was born in a country
of crenelated boundaries.
More twists and turns
More beaches per human
than any other offering.
The sea gave life itself.
Then I came to a land with
 an area of eight million
square kilometres. Whew.
How did I ever find you?
Infinite ecology and
more land bits and types
than an exploded bomb.
Didn't always know
where you were
in body and in mind
Until I redesigned
RADAR into a female
friendly version of itself.
I always had heat detection
And electrically charged
molecules on many
occasions, often bordering
close to dangerous.
I found curious landforms
A spectrum of climates
Reefs rivers and lakes
And the infinite sea.
We dragged anchor

on rare occasions
I couldn't find you
The wind blotted
everything from view.
But the powder rust
always fell away
And you were there
My Anchor.

AUNTY'S DOG

He's smart and inhabits her brain
Her molecules are almost his with
 doggy ideas on needs and wants.
Whimsical words slip Aunties lips
Perfectly interpreted with what
 pleases him. Complex sentences
 will be picked over for meaning
And if pleasure is not availed now
Then the limp comes back!

A once old injury taught him
 that sympathy comes in spades.
If the world regresses taking him
 without his God given rights,
Then the limp comes back.

He's loyal, rabidly clinging in fact.
He has evolved an attraction
To cling like a wrecker's magnet.
Even a tyre lever wont prize him
 loose from her heated lap.
Telepathy is one of his major skills.
Aunty anticipates his every need
 and should she fail at ninety-three
Then the limp comes back.

Usually, she knows his subtle wants
And his face reflects a winning smile
 of comfort, peace and cleverness,
And for a moment in time, he sleeps.

Then the limp lies dormant.
But only when he sleeps.
Then the limp comes back.

SUN BIRDS

Such intimacy.
They tweet and chatter
Knowing their lives continue
Creating a nest to love.

They find and feel the world
Joining parts of themselves
To weave a nest from a memory
Of such beautiful precision.

Eggs and young come and go.
Some to fly with the wind and
some into the belly of a snake.
Nature takes its course.

Seasons change, the young
are gone. The parents, a brief
hiatus, then a genetic memory
Nudges them to do it all again.

MISSING YOU

The frozen grass
A minus four frost.
Trying to stay warm
Without you with me.
I fed the shaky sparrows
Love needs some kind of outlet.
'Rats of the air', you once laughed.
I'm not sure who is the rat this morning
With me alone hugging a frozen body, no fire
Or heater and only a slight shiver of warm memories.

INFINITESIMAL

In
Normal
Fine
Increments
Nothing
Implies
Time
Especially
Size
In
Minute
Allotted
Lengths.

MYSTIC MEETING

How was I to know that you would go?
Time had moved, but deceptively slow.
Even with the strength of life in you
Some years even the months were few.
No farewells, no pomp, no thoughts
Of game plans or a battle to be fought.
An exit, an end, no hope of foreseeing.
You died. Lost, from the pleasure of being.
I know somewhere we had met before.
Pākehā landings or the Māori wars?
Were we souls passing by in the night,
Just checking in on a passing flight?
Mystical folk of mountains and sea
Perhaps we were Patupaiarehe,
making houses from the swirling mist
that curled around us in a soulful kiss.
Whatever your business on this cold land
You dealt chaos from a memorable hand.

THE SUN

We looked into the sharp rays of the sun.
We cackled, 'It makes everyone equal.'
Sharp pricks on our retinas burnt the scene.
We are all black in crisp harsh silhouette.
Bob and Meg, hand in hand, were black.
They were burnt on my green eyes forever
To watch them together move into the sun
Two-dimensional moving fluid cut-outs.
An impossible trick. He an Aboriginal
And she a pale blond headed memory.

TURMERIC IN OIL

Swirling in waves
Round and about
In sleek coalescence
Yellow to richness
Round and about
In busy enfolding
Mixing with no plan
Except moving atoms
Of unseen uniting
Turmeric in oil
Deepening in yellow
Coats the ingredients
With coloured excesses
The swirl of the oil
The dance of the day
Dinner is looming
With wands of utensils
Round and around
Turmeric in oil
Mingling with purpose
Glowing with goodness
Not sparing colour
A world of its worth
Medicine forever
And never forgotten
Beautifully dancing
Like turmeric in oil
Swirling in waves

WISH BONE IN WAITING

In a rare but timely cleaning frenzy.
I unearthed a relic of a former feast.
A wish bone, dry brittle and delicate.
I imagine cockroach nibbles cleaning
Your cloak of fine white sparse tissue.
A hopeful meal nibbled to perfection.

What does one do? Not a soul around
To link little fingers to snap the bone.
I could break it but then I would win.
That's hardly cricket. I'll conjure an
 inner alter ego. The ego can be the
Right hand and I will be the left.

Some egos don't deserve the time of day
That's enabling or so say those without sin.
Don't give away a wish they might abuse.
It might ignite negative energy, a backlash.
So, who deserves or needs a special wish?
Perhaps brittle Skye with her insecurities.

Her savage distrust for all things living.
A wish bone once lived. It's so dead now.
Would she find that safe in her cocoon?
I think it's best for someone more robust.
David. He's a bully but he can fix things.
Would he try to fix a shattered bone?

So, who needs a wish? Ah! Little Debbie.
So small. She's vacant and bewildered.

Poor little soul. Everyone's loss and regret.
She could wish for love and an exalted life.
I grasp the wishbone and pull with two hands.
Right side Debbie and the left side for me.

SNAP. I look in dismay. I have the bigger half.
Shall I take my prize or humbly give it away?
If Debbie is to have the exalted life she needs,
I wish for all the love on Earth to set her free.
Here's to all the lost and lonely souls as well
And know none of you will ever end in Hell.

SLEEP

Let your thoughts sink deeply
On any likely love story
Dancing wildly in the fading light
Supplications to the dreams of night.
Where spirits wander, teasing and
Switching the sagas to nightmares
Where variable weather unleashes
Random edits, film like, throwing
Blasts of humour, a charge of hope
A splash of horror or a deluge of love.
Your soul teases the calculating frames
Sacking your nightly journeys on a whim.
Conjure jewellers rouge, like pixie dust
On night horrors. Remember, like the sun
It brightens the gem. Rough or otherwise.
Sleep justly and well.

MY BOTANY PROFESSOR

She sipped peach plonk.
A wine so sweet and sickly.
Delicately sipped while she wrote
Papers of research and discoveries,
The likes I yearned to do.
I tried by chance a term paper.
My brain swum in whirls.
Sunlight peppered the page
And Fibonacci got lost in translation.
Then genetics and reproduction
Devolved with peculiar adaptations
Ecology was not sweet wine adaptive.
Surely science needs a brain loosened
At the lips. Gleeful to cut corners
With peach plonk rhetoric.
An unfettered view from the top,
A brain devoid of helpful hang-ups,
Careless with rigidity and research.
'Out of left field,' I hear.
'Out of left ear,' I see.
It's my right brained ear that knows
How to blend the writing symphony.
Mutations and time and more time.
Then I will show that angiosperms
Blossomed before the fall.

MY UNCLE IN SPRING

There are times when nothing is there.
Then a breeze sneaks in dragging the sun
in small slivers of remembering.
Glimpses of another era. He smiles.
A long crazy smile for times gone by.

Does he see the lucerne, oats and barley
rippling golden across his farm?
His wife, now gone, surfaces in vignettes.
'Ethel sure looked funny, wet as a shag.'
He rumbles with mirth as the sprinkler
continues its watery job on his flowers.

I'm hungry Lovey. How's Phyllis today?
'She's dead again this month,' I say with
sleepy syntax. I sit like an ornament
And play happy families while he chats
About dogs, chooks, tractors and loves
of his life that he remembers so dearly.

His world spins around. Colours cascade
And blend in tune with this lazy day.
Happy we sit, eat, laugh and be company,
In a universe where often, nothing is there
But today mimics a landscape of love.

AFTER GLOW

I once saw an old soul.
I knew it by her glow.
Not the colour or form
But an offering of spirit.
A radiance of knowledge
A life of molecules,
Vibrating their own story.
They could be catching
If you knew how to catch.
You might read her life
With no need for words
To love in a lover's realm.

THE USUAL SUSPECTS

When legless and intoxicated,
mostly in another's eyes.
Staggering lame and arrogant
To a fate of waning liquor and
smoke be not a substitute.
You demand another drink
And ignore the heartless care
in another's face. Fools they be.
Idiots in the bleary face of things.
Food! An anathema to a full gut,
Already bloated with grapes of rot.
Another drink wont seal one's fate
As will temper and intolerance.
Friendships now stretched too late
in the merry rush for enlightenment

SUNDAY WALKING

Sunday walking. Ice cold and alive.
I walk by a tall fence
Pinewood, seeping, not sap
But the bone warming allure
Of wood smoke and food.

A fragrance of meat,
Heated to perfection
With kumara and cabbage.
No sausage-sizzle this
Or pot boil on the stove.

Like teasing tendrils
The aroma migrates
Down-wind through cracks
Conjuring a memory
Of a world gone by.

Youthful play, near naked
Swimming like eels writhing
In a watery land of two halves
Where we were one with
A world born to our souls.

Back then our lives differed.
Cast out to the land of ferns
Until the wily smells of food
Always lured us home.
Trapped in a time warp of
Fun, family, friends and a hāngī.

LEARNING TO DANCE AGAIN

For Morgan

Life loses another round
Through the grey unfolding
Of many unfinished journeys.
Having wrestled the map
Of dubious destinations
Weathering drought and storms
And roads of curious options
The choreography falls over
And the waltz is no more.
Buto like, we freeze and wait.

The kids are skateboarding the town
The cockies are screeching their glee
As they dump missiles on the houses.
Turkeys programmed to kick and scrape
All show a constancy we wish for.
People like checkers can only start play
When the board is full. No gaps please.
You must learn the game of necessary
Presence as we are too brittle to allow
Your foolhardy crazy acting to stop.
It is us who will miss your edgy life
Of crazy with dashes of virtuosity.
Our memories will stumble
With the awesome dance of life
While we beat out a rhythm
In a direction vaguely right.

'So, to you all I give a compass
And a wind to set your sail,
And a special joke from me
Your sextant's in the mail.'

COMMUNION

A black man stood at my doorway
And cast an eye towards the hills
Of lush rainforest, dripping
And steaming from the morning rain.
With all the load of grief,
His hat clutched raggedly to his heart
He offered up the niceties of the day.
His idiosyncratic car and kids
The mosquitos and their sharp
Reminders of another reality,
Until the real force of his visit
Spilled into the fresh jungle air
Soothing the knitting of his heart
And wringing hand that fell open,
Vulnerable as a flower
To touch my arm and convey
Unspoken words, his brother's death.

LONE GRAVE

A slab of stone circled with chain
Defines your lonely presence.
A safety net in times of death
Saving you from the living.
Your outlying grave
Alone in a back street's
Nature strip of grass
That the council murders
And exposes you again.
An object for vandals.

Often when the sun is warming
Your grave and the quiet air
Trembles a mirage of memory.
I imagine your life. Sweetly short?
Was it happy? Filled with optimism?
A painless death? Who did you leave?
Rest easy in the pulse and chemistry
Of an Earth that will remember you
As I will in hope yet sadly, ignorance.

LIKE CHOCOLATE FOR LOVE

Love. That elusive quality
A twilight sunshine state.
Where a lover's world is neither
Blind, brown or troubled slate.

A glance a smile a caffeine wink
To a lone and choc-less heart
Sends mobs of lawless butterflies
Fat cupids without their darts.

Love is too ephemeral
In such a busy life
So, add two loves in one
A chocolate coated wife.

However, life is not so simple
Though chocolate helps a lot
Washed down in rich dark mocha
And a rum and coffee tot.

If love comes treading softly
With a hint of bittersweet
Smoothness and some sweetness
The love's more than a treat.

If you like a bit of colour
From white to heavy tan
It's life's ultimate indulgence.
Dark chocolate coated man.

TOURISM

My work was simple.
I looked after birds and sold
The right to see them.
I worked at the market
And smiled effusively
Because the tourists
Are on holiday and want
Their adventures and buoyed spirits
To be condoned and unthreatened.

I smile and joke a thousand times
Amidst their happy requirements.
They always laugh.
The Japanese so neat
With perfect fitted shorts
And perfect fitted bodies
Where gold clasps and chains
Declare exorbitant brands.
Schooled in excellence
They count their money
With biblical deliberation.
Their English easily recognised.
'Two Adul Plea' and 'Tankyou'
And with perfect inscrutability
They smile too and nod
Its catching and like Boobies
We bob and tip our separation.

The New Zealanders
So close yet far away

Don't have to tell me
How they 'putched their
Tint in a dup', or how
They love our 'fush and chups'.
Because they say they are from
Ngāruawāhia or Taranaki and
Have flightless birds. I smile.
Traitor to my heritage.
I'm a Kiwi too.

The English. They do wear
Sensible shoes and sensible voices.
I admire their spareness of movement.
They don't flap. Perhaps their survival
Back packs won't permit it.
They do have several bird books.
Binoculars buried within.
They play the game.
The search is on with childlike joy.
The prize is to find every bird
And declare the unlisted species
We only released that morning.
Such enthusasm supported
When they smile so regally.

The Americans enthusiastically panting.
Show excess fat marinated in sunscreen.
They have more jokes per pound of flesh
Than any other race and their money
American origami as bill folds blossom.
The men are jocularly trusting and display
 A gentlemanliness their partners condone.

The Germans and Swiss
So brown, blond and confident
Read the information with precision.
Their money, any size is prompt
As is their, 'two persons'.
They smile charmingly, so please
Is superfluous. They can be made
To laugh. The birds, you see, steal earrings.
Any hunk of blue-eyed Aryan flesh
Laughs outrageously at my futile concern.
'Mein Gott. I do not wear earrings.' Haha.
And when I hear a badly disguised
'Oh, lucky I left mine at home.'
It's a middle aged Ocker bloke on holiday
Who gets an adoring thump from his wife.
'You silly Bugger.'

The Aussies love the birds.
They know how these birds
Mirror their heritage.
The sunburnt vistas
The green rolling planes
And the lush tropical wetness
Of this adored holiday.
The wildlife is part of their soul.
Yes, they regret destruction
And unconsciously wish to imbue
The calm that later years bring.
Rejuvenated they leave
And smiling is easy.

MEETING MY MOTHER

I got married once.
I took the Beau to
 meet his mother-in law.
She was on her best behaviour.
The Beau was a scientist.
He had an accent, American.
To Mum this was a boost
to his gene pool, I gathered.
He must be very smart
She sounded impressed,
based on nothing at all.
I had to leave these two,
for a few hours together.
The dentist was needed.
I wondered if the Beau
would resort to gagging,
strangulation or insanity.
The dentist was doubly
displeasing. I raced home.
Nervous and exhausted.
How did you and Mum get on?
I asked with fake nonchalance.
Absolutely fine. He smiled.
She talked all day
And I read a book.

NIGHT DIVE ON THE REEF

The cloak of night sets in
Luminescence flashes.
When we plunge through
A liquid sheet, into a black
Watery world with stars.
A scientist, torch in hand
Blasts the unwary denizens
With a bright yellow beam
Cascading over the scene
To catch the naked polyps
In all their flashy glory
Dressed in colours that seem
Impossible to believe.
We saw the night shift
We felt so privileged
With imprints on our brains
That will remain forever.

THE DRESSMAKER

1950's untimely and ill conceived.
A girl who likes engines.
Dad an engineer
Mum a war bride
Who took a man's job.
As Men defended hearth and home.
Mum ran the farm
Charmed old tractors
Stuttering Model A's
And a two wheeled Indian.
She was a welder too.
Aunty ran and reeled
The local cinema when not
Driving a traction engine
At the coal face.
When I came along
My small head and eager
Snout was now sub-bonnet.
I could pass spanners
Screw drivers and hold
Small things steady.
The engines displayed
Their small part glory.
Then Dad exclaimed.
Young woman, go inside.
I thought Tea. Sure Dad.
No. Just go away. An order!
Confused, I searched his face.
The boys, head down, bums up
Well-oiled wrenched away.

'What do you want?' I asked.
I just want you to go away.
Because? The bomb shell.
The boys might swear
And worse, I might too.
You already do. I whispered.
Go. He pointed like a Greek God.
I stomped off and the boys stayed
With their potty mouths.
Me with my muddy brain
Exited garage left.
He suggested I become
A dress maker, a seamstress.
To fix things he said blandly.
A machine of minutiae.
So, my first career was just that.
My Mother's heritage lost,
To time and Men.

THE NIGHT IS OVER

Bali High Club. Auckland 1964

Sublime and eighteen.
A secret Goddess
To be admired
By old men.
Her usual audience
At this special hour.

Dance was her brain
Her body was pure
Her body in the dance
Was seen as theirs.
A dichotomy of pleasures
Hers to give, theirs to take.

The old men would lean
Into the stage, all eyes.
Eager as puppy dogs
Hoping for a treat.
The stage a small slab
Of raised wood blocks.

They ogled her, Juanita.
The name was love of
Gypsy music, slinky tango
And hot snappy flamenco.
Her skin a gloss of brown
Her eyes green as envy.
Hair with no control

Dark curled and savage.
It found its own space
To create total abandon.
The dance was suggesting
A shared heartbeat rhythm.

Her legs were fine delights,
Her dress split to the waist,
Ankles, thighs in impossible
Dimensions, as groans ignite
In various timbres and sighs
To saturate the thickening air.

Her dress of olive-green satin
Floated like a delicate shy shawl
Well trained and expertly used.
Her right foot would vibrate
Tap style at an impossible speed.
An unearthly tremor of lust.

Abandon was now creeping in.
Her eyes still alert and focused
Sweep across the old men
And smile in anticipation.
Her lips would boldly throw kisses
As sensuous as her clinging dress.

Her eyes would dip like doves' wings.
As she navigated her space of boards.
Her stage a small space she understood,
The floor the walls and four fat poles
A treat, a prop yet to be molested.

The dance was only halfway there.

A final change the music hit a high
And changed to a slow, slinky melody.
Gently spinning like a ballerina
The flamenco dress held by one clasp
Easily released to spin away from.
A ruffle of satin floated to her feet.

Not naked but scanty in black lace
Knickers and tiny top girded with her
Grandmothers' ancient crystal beads.
Gifted to wear to church with a lemon
Flocked nylon knee length dress.
And patent leather super shiny shoes.

If she had known, would Gran
Have smiled and applauded at
Her taste in design or rolled over
In her grave laughing fit to bust.
She made it to ninety-nine plus,
Saw wars famine and hardships.

Free of satin, her spine folded
Down her back to her firm legs
Where peeping coquettishly
she would bend between them
and wink at the old men who
moaned at her contortions.

Disaster, the spell is broken.
The gauche simple odd job boy

Crashes into the turntable
Screech of nerves and her music.
It skips and jumps but settles in a
Different place in time and space.

She smiles and ends with flips
And contortions then time is up.
The dance is over the cheers start.
She sinks slowly into a final fold
Of supplication showing her thanks.
The audience united in a roar of joy.

CANCER CURE

Raratonga, Cook Islands

I left the field
Of limp grass and
Yellow drying flowers.
It was winter.
No ice or bitter winds
But cool sea breeze
And tepid ocean.
I walked the walk
You had no strength for.
Cancer, a creeping death.
You did make it to
The bottom of the garden
To the ocean beyond.
We were in the Islands
A Pacific paradise where
Beaches should be illegal.
Their beauty a panacea,
The Doctor, handsome
Power in his medicine
Strength in desire of a cure.
A special elixir, untested
Power in trust and belief.
Chemotherapy, a backup.
Sorry about your hair.
It was white anyway.
You were never given
To seductions and charm.
Pragmatic and sensible.

Did the elixir stand a chance?
The chemo distorted you
Until the cancer did its job.
Your final rest by the sea,
In a graveyard now closed.
Being wrapped in ferns
Broad leaf shrubs and grass
And soft mosses cushioning
A gentle cycle of renewal.

HALLOWEEN

It is one edgy strange night
Where horrors are permitted
Under scary masks with mock
Evil intent and potty language.
Trick or treat as the can rattles
For any offers as the veil thins
To placate spirits on the move.
The kids, natural terrors attack
Laughing through a mock game
Where little kids taste the power
Of treats and melted chocolate.
While the night holds its breath
As edgy sleep steals the children
To wake with the sun and gripes.
Delayed horrors of a sugar kick.

GOODNIGHT

Paint yourself on a still dark sky.
Your medium is your heart's desire.
Are you a splatter of a million stars
Merging with a strip of milky way?
Or constellations in love, so grouped
With family and many special friends.
The sky forever, and now, your map
Of dreams, compositions of hues
So subtle your brain now succumbs
while sinking into the black of night
a million friends to visit in a dream
a million animals to have as pets
it's all yours tonight. Sleep tight!
 And as Granny would surely shout.
"Don't let those pesky bed bugs bite."

About the Author

Janice Starck is a non-fiction author, poet and playwright living in the rainforests of far north Queensland, Australia. She has previously worked as a marine biologist, high school science teacher, wildlife curator, tour guide, dancer, documentary film maker, photojournalist and seamstress. Originally from New Zealand, for many years she lived in the Pacific Islands on a marine research vessel. She didn't want to include that she has previously held the world underwater endurance record and was once Miss Waikato Youth Club Queen, but her family wrote this bio and thought it was too funny not to mention

www.ingramcontent.com/pod-product-compliance
Lightning Source LLC
Chambersburg PA
CBHW062053290426
44109CB00027B/2819